GOD'S GRACE ALONE

God's Grace Alone

by
STARR ROGERS

RESOURCE *Publications* • Eugene, Oregon

GOD'S GRACE ALONE

Copyright © 2020 Starr Rogers. All rights reserved. Except for brief quotations in critical publications or reviews, no part of this book may be reproduced in any manner without prior written permission from the publisher. Write: Permissions, Wipf and Stock Publishers, 199 W. 8th Ave., Suite 3, Eugene, OR 97401.

Resource Publications
An Imprint of Wipf and Stock Publishers
199 W. 8th Ave., Suite 3
Eugene, OR 97401

www.wipfandstock.com

PAPERBACK ISBN: 978-1-7252-7688-8
HARDCOVER ISBN: 978-1-7252-7689-5
EBOOK ISBN: 978-1-7252-7690-1

Manufactured in the U.S.A.   JUNE 3, 2020

This book is dedicated to my beloved children, grandchildren and to my Lord and savior.

The thief comes only to steal and kill and destroy; I have come that they may have life, and have it to the full."

—John 10:10

July in Alabama is scorching. It'll make you feel like you're being strangled just standing on the front porch. The drone of cicadas and crickets filled the air. The dust from the dirt road would kick up from a dull breeze and give life a sepia tone. If you were my age you were supposed to be outside playing because houses in the 60s didn't have air conditioning. I was on my bike and pedaling as fast as I could, until I couldn't feel my legs, for a different reason. I was trying to stop thinking about what happened at my grandmother's house. I was trying to stop thinking about both of my uncle's hands reaching for me and dragging me underneath the house and away from the light. They were tearing my pants off, they were covering my mouth, they were slipping fingers inside of me. One held me down while the other got what he wanted. One of them brought out a matchstick and made it disappear inside of me. They left in a hurry when they heard someone hollering for them but I stayed put. I was torn open. A small animal that had been feasted on and left to bleed out slowly. I pretended that I was dead below the house. I was 8 years old.

My mother, Ruby, got pregnant with me very young and her mother threw her out of the house. She was ashamed but that was odd since my grandmother was the town tramp. She was also meaner than a rattlesnake and hated my guts because I was my father's child. My parents got married but didn't feel anything for each other. They got married because that's what you're supposed to do if you have a baby on the way and life at home was always chaotic. Both of them were cheating on each other any chance they could. Daddy worked and my mother picked up odd jobs here and there. I always felt like I wasn't wanted, like I was a burden on them. My daddy was rarely home. He was out fishing or hunting or seeing other women. My mother had men coming over to our house. One afternoon I was playing in the front yard when a friend of my daddy's came and picked me up and started feeling my breasts. He put his hand down my pants right there in broad daylight. I don't know why he was doing this but I felt ashamed and I didn't tell anyone. He was there to bring my mother a birthday present. They were sleeping together.

In 1967 my mother was pregnant again. I didn't know it at the time but the child wasn't my daddy's. The father was his best friend, an old fishing buddy. My sister, Tammy, was born on August 7th and, to make it even more wonderful, she was brought home on my birthday. I was so excited to have my own babydoll to play with. I'd just turned 10 years old.

Things were getting worse between my parents. I tried to spend as much time as I could at my paternal grandmother's house. I couldn't wait for Friday to come so I could go to Granny's for the weekend. She lived in Eclectic, Alabama. A town so small that if you blinked you would miss it. It would've qualified as a one-stoplight town if they had one stoplight. Dirt roads and empty fields were the only scenery. In the summer I didn't miss home at all. The only things I missed were my little sister and my dog Penny. When my mother and daddy got tired of shouting and couldn't stand each other anymore they divorced. No one was upset and it was a relief more than anything. My mother got custody of my sister and daddy got me and that meant I got to go live with Granny since he was working all the time and couldn't look after me. After the divorce, my mother turned into a nomad. She refused to put roots down anywhere for long. There was this deep restlessness in her. She moved when the rent came or when she found a new man. My sister never knew what a home was and neither did I but I only lived with her until I was 12. We never had a close, loving relationship. I knew that my sister was the favorite and the 2 of them were so alike it was scary. I always felt like I had to raise myself. I couldn't handle not knowing where I was gonna lay my head at night and I knew that wouldn't change with my mother.

Granny bought a trailer in the early 70s and put it in my aunt Nell's yard. She was my daddy's little sister. Granny had an upholstery shop in my aunt's garage. She could do anything with a roll of cloth and made most of my clothes. Granny and granddaddy were divorced before I came along. She married again and when they got divorced her second husband shot her. She was sitting on the back porch one night with my great grandmother and they heard footsteps crunching in the gravel. Granny reached up to turn on the porch light and when she did she saw him standing there with his gun pointed right at her. He was aiming for her heart but because of how she was positioned turning the light on he missed his target. He took off running up the road to where he parked his car. It took the deputies all night to find him. Granny went to the hospital and so much damage had been done to her that she had to wear a colostomy bag for the rest of her life. Her ex-husband went to prison.

My mother and sister were living with a woman named Mrs. Wadsworth. She was also divorced and had three children that her ex had custody of. She got pregnant by a nineteen year old and that's what broke up her marriage. I missed my sister terribly but I didn't go see her because of the chaos in their household.

God's Grace Alone

When I turned 15 Granny said it was okay for me to date. My first boyfriend looked just like Glen Campbell and I was crazy about him. He worked at the dairy barn right next to our house. He had to get up at 3 in the morning to milk the cows. I stayed up late to listen to him blow his horn as he passed by our house. The horn sounded like a wolf whistling out there in the dark. I got such a kick out of that. I shared a bed with Granny and I loved laying there and talking with her. I didn't care what we talked about because everything was so easy with her. When I thought of home I thought of her. She was the only one I'd ever known. The only thing I didn't like was when my uncle would come over. He was my daddy's little brother. He watched me like a hawk. If I was alone in the house he would try to touch me on the arm or push up against me. I felt like an animal backed into a corner when he was near. I spent as much time as I could in the bathroom during his visits because that was the only room with a lock. Daddy wasn't there much but that wasn't new. He was so self-absorbed and had to be perfect and his idea of perfect didn't include me.

After a while I started feeling like I was in the way at Granny's. She was getting older and my aunt and uncle never really liked me living there. I became an afterthought. A toy once cherished and now put up on the shelf to collect dust. At the age of 16 I got married. I thought that would make the situation better for everyone involved.

I met James Taunton at the private school we both attended. He was a football player and we only went with each other for a few months. In 1973 we got married at a tiny country church in Tallapoosa county. I borrowed a wedding dress from my friend Sharon Jackson. All of the flowers cost $25 but my daddy still complained about that. My mother didn't attend and my daddy showed up with one of his girlfriends while his other girlfriend was escorted by my soon to be brother in law. I don't even remember what the preacher said but I remember not being in love. This is what I had to do to get away from a bad situation. We had a one night honeymoon at the Holiday Inn because we were borrowing my brother in law's car and we had to get it back to him the next day. We didn't have a car or our own home. We had to move in with his mother and brother. That was a living hell. No privacy and his family was the wildest, angriest bunch of folks you'd ever meet. James' father had a dictator's temper that he passed onto his children. He beat his wife mercilessly and when he was through with her he took it out on the kids. He was a full blown alcoholic, all of his sons were as well, and cussed and drank like it was going out of style. I remember hearing hollering and groaning outside and only to walk out and find James and one of his brothers fist fighting. The whole town knew about them and overlooked their ways.

Eventually we got our own place. An old trailer with walls like a cardboard box. We baked in the summer and froze our tails off in the winter. Most of the time we only had food for one meal a day. James was working at a landscaping business owned by his family and saved up enough money for us to buy another trailer that wasn't on his parents land and our own car. The hard times seemed like they would go on forever. The power, gas or water was constantly being turned off. Sometimes we had to siphon gas out of our neighbors cars after they went to bed so James could make it to work in the morning. For months we lived off of instant mashed potatoes and hotdog chilli and we stole our toilet paper from gas stations. It wasn't long before James started hanging out with friends after work. They drank and smoked dope and did the usual things that men did when they were with other men which meant they acted like idiots. I wanted to leave but had nowhere to go and nobody to turn to. I was young and lonely and in over my head. One morning there was a knock at the door and standing there was a salesman from Liberty National. His name was Larry Finney. He was 10 years older than me and tall and handsome and well-dressed and his scent would put you in a trance. His hair had receded into a cul de sac around his head. His mustache was dark and full. His eyes were just as dark and shot through with sadness. Even when he smiled he looked haunted. I let him in the trailer and we talked for hours. I didn't buy any insurance but that didn't stop the morning visits. Being around him was the only time I didn't feel like loneliness was going to eat me alive. I was slowly falling in love with him. After 5 months I let him make love to me and soon after that I found out I was pregnant. I knew it wasn't my husband's. When I gave birth my daughter she looked just like Larry. We named her Hope and I passed her off as my husband's child. The affair continued.

We carried on this affair for ten years and then I got pregnant again. We decided to get an abortion this time. I couldn't let my sin find me out. I had a life and I couldn't let it come crashing down around me so I destroyed an innocent life. The pain was excruciating. I felt like I had my guts ripped out. I felt like I was walking around with my nerves exposed. I ignored the pain because I needed to keep seeing this man. I thought he would leave his wife and we could be happy but he wouldn't. She was an R.N. and that was his meal ticket. He could do whatever he wanted with his money while she paid all of the bills and took care of their two children. When he got me pregnant again he drove me to the abortion clinic in Montgomery and stayed in the car and smoked. When it was over he drove me back to my car which was parked behind Eastdale mall. Larry was working as the manager of Jarman's shoes inside of the mall. One of his employees was waiting on him. Her name was Lisa and she was 19 years old and nothing to look at. Larry wouldn't hire any men to work at the store and I found out later that the two of them were fooling around. She was obsessed with Larry. She got my phone number and started calling my house at least 20 times a day and would hang up whenever I answered. This was before Caller I.D. so I had to call the phone company and have them put a trace on my line. I wrote down every time there was a call and the date. After several weeks they found that the calls were coming from the shoe store. I confronted Larry about this and he swore nothing was going on between them. The phone company contacted the main office of the shoe store and Larry and Lisa were reprimanded and then it came to light that they were both stealing credit cards from customers. They charged $1500 and went on a shopping spree. He was also paying for her to go to art school. Larry never could hold a job for long if he had to handle money. Larry's daddy got him out of that mess but Larry's father was just as crooked as his son. He was a womanizer that masqueraded as the deacon of the church he helped build. He slept with a different woman every night of the week but always showed up at church on Sunday with his wife beside him. Larry learned a lot of lessons from that cold-hearted man.

Larry told me that he was going to leave his wife while she was on vacation with his children. He was just going to pack up and go. He wanted me to leave my husband too so that's what I did. I was a fool for him. I gathered up my things while James was at work and I left. Larry put me and our daughter up in a run down hotel. I didn't know what we were supposed to do but wait. Our daughter watched TV while I kept my eyes darting back and forth between the clock on the wall and the door. We were there for 3 days. When Larry did show up he told me that he couldn't leave his wife because of their kids. I said what about our daughter but he didn't answer. We went back home and James had been looking for us. It was hell at our house for a long time after that. James wouldn't let me out of his sight. I had to account for every minute of every day. I was cussed out and barked at. I considered changing my name to slut because that was all I heard. He made me go and apologize to my mother in law for running off and being a whore and then he made me do the same thing with my Granny. That just about killed me. Looking her in the eye and actually saying these words. I hated him for that. I would never forgive him. My daily routine consisted of waiting on him hand and foot. Jumping when he said jump and being at his beck and call. At night I was his sex slave. I was living but I wasn't alive. I followed orders because that's what I had to do to have a place to lay my head. I had no other options. My own family didn't want to have anything to do with me. My daddy told me I had embarrassed him and that he was ashamed of having me for a daughter. Hearing him say that was like having my heart flattened with a hammer. I felt like trash. I heard from Larry again a few months later. He kept telling me how sorry he was and promised me that we were going to have a life together. I believed him. I had to. I had nothing else to believe in.

I got divorced from James. I couldn't take living like a beaten animal. Larry was still with his wife but kept insisting that it wouldn't be much longer until we could be together. He started showing me houses that he wanted to buy for us. I found out that I was pregnant again for the 3rd time and when I told Larry he said he couldn't take on another child at this point. I went to Birmingham to have it done. The whole ordeal was a blur. I remember being put to sleep and when I woke up I was sitting in a recliner in a room full of other women in the same predicament surrounding me. I was too numb to cry. My soul was being carved out with a dull knife. Innocent blood was on my hands. I could wash my hands a billion times and they'd never come clean. I returned home and spent most of my days weeping. I couldn't keep my emotions steady. I thought about killing myself. I thought that was the only way I could get peace from the turmoil.

Larry rented me an apartment around the corner from his job. He wanted me there when he got off of work and he wanted dinner cooked. He'd eat and watch TV and we'd have sex and then he'd go home to his wife and kids. I started to see the common threads between the two men that I was caught between. They both needed someone to control. They both needed me under their thumbs. I got pregnant again and, of course, Larry wasn't happy. I made another trip to Birmingham but this time there were protestors outside of the clinic. The air was tense and their shouting was overwhelming. A security guard came to escort me into the building but one voice cut through the roar. This woman called me a baby killer. Another tried to pray with me. The security guard pried me away from her and pulled me inside. The doors of the clinic closed and all of those voices trying to save me and this unborn child were silenced. When I went back home I was even more dead inside.

Larry had gotten behind on the rent. He wrote a check but it bounced. He had a gambling problem that I didn't know about. I was evicted and all of the furniture was repossessed. He had been working at a Ford dealership but got fired because he was stealing gas tickets. The dealership would give the salesmen gas tickets to put in the cars that they drove. They could use any car on the lot to take home or anywhere else they wanted. They were only supposed to use the tickets sparingly but Larry had stolen over $2500 worth of tickets. The company found out about it and fired him. They were going to prosecute him but his daddy gave him the money, like he always did. Larry was panicked over it. He kept saying he was going to go to Greenland to avoid going to jail. I don't know what he thought he was going to do there. He had been taking all of these pills. A friend of his was a pharmaceutical salesman and supplied Larry with all kinds of pills and he stayed in this constant fog. The divorce from James was finalized in 1987. As soon as enough time had passed I married Larry. I didn't tell any of my family and only our daughter knew. The old familiar feeling of a funeral loomed over the ceremony. Even Larry's mother said so. I thought it would've been one of the happiest days of my life but I felt like I was being read my last rites. This was only a prelude of what was to come.

We didn't have a honeymoon. In fact, after we were married, we never went anywhere. We only had one car and Larry had to take it to work. I got pregnant shortly after the wedding and I was so excited. I thought we were going to start a family of our own but Larry was angry. He didn't want to raise another child. His teenage son lived with us and his daughter lived with her mother and that was enough for him. I was so far along that I had to go to Atlanta for the procedure. I was a puppet doing whatever this man wanted me to do. Larry took out a loan for the abortion because it cost $1000. He rented me a car for the trip but sent me there alone. I traveled with a heavy heart. My vision was obscured by tears. There was something different with this child. I couldn't explain it but I could feel it. I'd been down this road before and it was always agonizing but this trip was harder than the others.

When I got to the clinic and walked in the presence of evil was palpable. There were so many women, just like me, ready to destroy a beautiful life. I was having the saline amniocentesis. They do this particular procedure after 16 weeks. Labor is induced and then saline is injected to burn your baby to death. I couldn't shake the image of this little one writhing in pain and clawing to get out, to be saved. I went to talk with the counselor. She was a large framed black woman with the kindest eyes. In all of my trips I'd never talked with a counselor that seemed like they were genuinely concerned about me. They were all so cold and going through the motions. She told me that I didn't want to abort my baby before I even opened my mouth. I was inconsolable and she held me tight. There was a window behind her desk and she got up and pulled the curtains back. She told me to look at the dumpster that was outside. She told me that's where they were going to put my baby. I broke down. She told me to go back to Alabama and have this child. She hugged me again and she felt so warm and loving. It reminded me of being in my Granny's arms. When I left and went home, I knew that God had put an angel in that room to stop the slaughter. I told Larry that I was keeping this baby and that's when he showed me his wrath. He told me I was going to put the baby up for adoption and I finally put my foot down. I had let men run my entire life until this point but I wasn't budging with this. I told him hell no. I was keeping this baby no matter what. I managed to find a doctor who would take me as far along as I was. My sister went with me to my appointment and when the ultrasound was done I found out that I was having a boy. He was due in October. I couldn't wait to meet him. For the first time, in a long time, I was crying tears of joy. Larry was still furious. He wouldn't pay my doctor bills or let me buy anything for the baby or any maternity clothes for myself. My family had to do that. I was alone in this but I wouldn't waver. I was supposed to have this child. I could feel it in my marrow.

In October of 1988 my son was born. The labor was long and difficult and I only had my mother by my side. When it was over and they laid him on my chest I knew what true love was. It was the happiest moment of my life. I just stared at him and he reached his little hand up to touch my face. I never wanted to let him go. I couldn't believe God blessed me with a baby this wonderful after what I had done to my other children. Larry didn't come to the hospital until 3 days after our son was born. He didn't hold him or talk to him. All he wanted to know was what name I gave him. I called him Matthew. Larry's other two children, Anne and Todd, were with him. Anne despised me and stuck her nose up at everyone. She said Matthew was ugly and I wanted to slap her face off. I told them to all get out. I wanted to be alone and hold my precious boy. My mother, my daughter and James all came to visit me in the hospital. James was taking care of my daughter. He had to step up and be daddy because Larry wouldn't. My father and Larry's parents never came to see their grandchild. Despite all of this, I left the hospital with the hope that we would be okay and try to be a family.

Larry had a jealous streak a mile wide in him. He hated our son and wanted all of my attention for himself. The jealousy wasn't limited to only our son. Any man with a pulse was a threat to him. When our daughter got older and started to date he didn't want her boyfriends coming to our house because I might talk to them. If I went anywhere then he had to take me. He had the phone turned off. I couldn't have friends and the only neighbors were his parents. Our house was nestled on 280 acres of woods behind a locked gate. It was like living in an exiled kingdom. My love for my son made me forget all about my living situation. I wanted to make up for what I had almost done to him. The guilt consumed me. I would look at this baby and my heart would break over and over again. I thanked God for what He had given me.

Granny died suddenly. She had gone in for surgery on her colon. Ever since her gunshot all of those years ago she had problems with her bowels. When she was out of surgery she was on a gurney in the elevator and she had a heart attack. When she left she took what little family I had with her. She was more of a mother to me than my own mother. Nothing was the same after that. No more get-togethers on the 4th of July, no more Thanksgiving, no more Sunday dinners. We drifted apart and never managed to find each other again. All I had left were my memories of being in bed and talking with Granny late into the night. The glue that held us together was gone.

I was pregnant again. We used birth control but that didn't work. I had another daughter and we named her Ashley. Larry actually came to the hospital this time but he was only there in the physical sense. He would've rather been anywhere else in the world. He wouldn't hold her. He just sat there looking like he was going to cave in on himself. His lips were pursed tightly while he stewed in his anger. I had my tubes tied after that and I hoped this would finally make Larry happy. I'd gotten rid of all of my baby clothes before my second daughter came along. I didn't have anything to bring her home in except for a blanket. I thought the hospital would let me keep the shirt from the nursery but they wouldn't. She came home in a blanket and a diaper. I kept her covered up so no one would know.

My sister, Tammy, had given birth to her 3rd child a few months after my son was born. She had her first child at the age of 14. She never knew a stable life from living with my mother. They moved every time the rent was due and the men that my mother brought home were the scum of the Earth. Sherman, the man that my sister was pregnant by, wasn't any different. He only worked half the time and then he would beat my sister. She was a big girl and could've knocked his lights out but that wasn't in her. She was still a child herself. If she could've had it her way she would spend all day at the gas station playing on the Pac-man machine. They wrote bad checks all over town just to have enough food for the children. My mother worked herself to the bone trying to support them. Barely getting by seemed to be the story for everyone in my family.

Starr Rogers

I was at home one night with the kids when Larry's boss brought him home. He was working at the Hills and Brook's coffee company. He had been fired for stealing from the company. They didn't press charges but he had to pay back all of the money he took. He was out of work for 3 months and I had somehow gotten pregnant again. I couldn't believe it. Having my tubes tied was supposed to take care of that but I was in the same predicament. I had put on weight at the time and my periods had never been normal. I was in complete shock. My last child was born in 1992. I had another son named Andrew.

Things were terrible between Larry and I. I tried to make our marriage work and keep the family together but Larry was battling me at every turn. He was mean to the kids and complained about them nonstop. They couldn't make a peep without him raising Cain. With all of the drama at home, my sister was getting sick. She couldn't even fight off a cold. She was in and out of the hospital and the doctors couldn't find out what was wrong with her. After they had done every test they could think of she was given an AIDS test. It came back positive. Tammy had full blown AIDS. I remember the world standing still. I thought I'd never catch my breath again after hearing the news. She had contracted it through a blood transfusion when she had her second child. A drug addict had donated tainted blood to pay for another fix and my sister was the recipient. She lived only 9 more years after she contracted the disease. She wasted away to nothing. Her chest looked like the buzzards had picked it clean. Her skin was pulled tight over her bones. She was hooked up to an IV and a feeding tube. My mother took care of her when she wasn't working. I looked after her as well but with my kids and her kids all packed into that little house made it too hectic. Sherman hired a woman from down the street to look after Tammy. We found out later that he was sleeping with this woman and after my sister passed they got married and had children of their own.

Tammy died on June 2nd, 1993 in my mother's arms. Her body had to be taken to Birmingham to be embalmed because no funeral home in Montgomery would touch her. The funeral was heart-shattering. Her daughter, Lindsey, clung to the casket and called for her momma, her oldest son couldn't stop crying, but her middle child, the one she got the virus with, couldn't have cared less. He was absolutely his father's son. My mother resented him and, in a way, I did too. When the funeral was over she went back to my sister's house and Sherman was having a party. He was drinking beer and playing loud music. He was glad she was dead so he could move on with his new sweetheart. My mother had to get all of her things and move out of the house even though she was the one taking care of the family. I don't know how I made it out of this alive. I thought I was going to lose my mind. I felt so guilty for living, especially since I was 10 years older than her. I was hollowed out. Every day was a struggle after that. I had all I could take of Larry. He didn't come to the funeral and he was getting meaner by the day towards the children. They didn't want anything to do with him and the only reason he tolerated them was because I wouldn't let them go. All he wanted was me and him alone in this house and to be chained to his endless self-pity. I wanted out. I couldn't take being a prisoner for a second longer. I packed up and went to my ex-husband's house.

I put every ounce of energy into cleaning the house. I would clean the entire house only to clean it again an hour later. I was always restless. I started cutting the grass three times a week just to exhaust myself. That was how I coped. It took my mind off of thinking and if I started thinking I knew I was going to destroy myself. I couldn't let the gears in my head turn slightly. I would unravel if they did.

One morning I went to pick up my oldest daughter from school. I had to check her out in the office and I left Matthew in the car with my aunt Mary. It took forever to get her out of class and I was wondering what the hold up was. I found out that Larry was good friends with the principal and he told the office workers to let him know if I came to get my daughter. Larry was in Tallassee and I was in Wetumpka so I had to be stalled until he could get there. He found my car and took Matthew to his parents' house. He told me I wasn't getting my son back. I couldn't call the cops because he had as much right to Matthew as I did. I left without my son. I didn't figure Larry would keep him long. I knew Larry didn't want him but Larry knew how much I loved this little boy and this was his way of making me come back. I stood my ground even if it tore me up to leave my son.

For two months Matthew lived with Larry and I got him on the weekends. That's when I started to notice my baby wasn't how he used to be. He was such a happy boy but now this sadness lingered over him. I could feel that something wasn't right. When I took him home with me he would hug me and say, "Mommy, I missed you so." I cried harder than I ever had. He didn't want to be away from me at all. He would cling to me like I was all that was keeping him from drowning. I didn't know how true that was.

I continued to stay at James' house. I couldn't go back home. I didn't have anyone else. My mother was a wreck from Tammy's death and my daddy was ashamed of me and for 10 years we didn't speak. It didn't seem to bother him, but he never was the loving father type. I took care of my children the best way I could without support from Larry. I had to get on food stamps and most of their clothes came out of the Goodwill box. At times I felt like I couldn't go on. My heart was heavy and it seemed like my entire life was a series of unrelenting punches. God had blessed me with good babies though. They never gave me a minute's trouble and they pulled me through. I don't know where I would be if I didn't have them.

As Matthew got older he kept having bathroom issues. I couldn't figure out why this was happening until Matthew told me that Larry and his grandpa had been molesting him. They both sodomized him and touched him. Larry beat him everyday. Matthew told me about all of the nights he spent locked inside of the closet of his room because Larry didn't want to deal with him. Matthew was trapped in there and would scream and cry all night until eventually he passed out. He told me that at dinner Larry would cram food down his throat and force him to eat. Matthew was trying not to eat or drink because he knew he'd be in that little closet and he'd have to go to the bathroom but he wouldn't be able to. Guilt and anger overwhelmed me. I wanted nothing more than to kill Larry and his old man. I wanted to burn their properties to the ground and erase any sign that these awful people had ever been put on this Earth. When I confronted Larry he denied it, of course. He said Matt was making it up but I could look in my son's eyes and see the truth. He went from the happiest boy to looking like even mustering a smile hurt him. The signs were all there and I missed them completely. Matthew had always had trouble speaking. He was painfully shy and words seemed like they had to be pried out of him. I knew he needed to speak with someone so I took him to a therapist. Matthew told her about the sexual abuse and she had to report it to DHR. A social worker was sent to my house and she looked around to make sure the house was clean and that the kids were being taken care of. She found nothing wrong. The therapist started seeing Matthew once a week and she told me I could take Larry to court but Matt would have to be the one to tell everything that happened. Matt wasn't emotionally stable enough to do that. The thought of possibly seeing his father again made him panic. He also wanted to stop seeing the therapist because he felt like it wasn't helping. He said he was in there spilling his guts and she acted like he was talking about the weather. The guilt from all of this was unbearable. This man that I loved and had these children with was a monster. I wished for death on him and his father. I prayed for it. During all of this I found out that Larry's parents molested him. He told me that his mother would hold him down while his father preyed on him. I didn't know if he was telling the truth or trying to get sympathy out of me but the signs were in him too. All of those years living with that quiet rage in him but never being able to help or understand what it meant. That haunted look I'd seen in Matt had been in Larry from the beginning. His parents had turned him into a monster and that monster had gotten claws into my son. I couldn't reconcile any of this. My world stopped turning again.

I remarried James. I don't know why but I did. I was messed up from top to bottom. I was still seeing other men despite James bearing down even more with his possessive ways. He didn't trust me, he never would and I didn't care at this point. I thought a man could fix me and fill this hole that was growing wider by the day. I started walking at the park by my house at night when everyone was gone. I knew it was dangerous to be out there at night by myself but deep down I think I wanted something to happen to me. I was barely alive at this point. I was an empty shell that kept breathing for some reason.

There was a gas station across the street from the park and I would stop in there sometimes and talk to my friend who worked the register. One evening there was another man in there talking up a storm and then I noticed that I was seeing him all the time now. Whenever I went to talk to my friend he was there and before long he was showing up at the park. We walked and talked for hours. It wasn't like I was in any hurry to get home. Before long we were having an affair. I fell for this man almost as hard as I fell for Larry. His name was Mickey and from what I could tell he was a sweet man. It had been so long since anyone had been kind to me that it didn't take much for me to love him. I divorced James again in November of 2006. I didn't take anything from my marriage except my clothes, my children's clothes and an old car. I felt I deserved nothing. Mickey bought a trailer off an old dirt road that they used to use for drag racing and our front porch had a view of the state prison. I was Mickey's 4th wife. His first wife was the love of his life and they divorced after 6 months after they dated for 5 years. His second marriage also lasted 6 months. He was married to his 3rd wife for 23 years and they had one son. She left him for another man when she got tired of him drinking and smoking dope and hanging out with his friends all hours of the night. Mickey had a 30 year drug habit but he quit when she wanted to get a divorce. The damage was done, though, and she wanted to move on with her life. I would feel her pain in a few years.

Mickey had started out such a good hearted man but as time went on he complained more and more. He griped about me not working the most. I hadn't had a job since the early 80s but I managed to find one at the First United Methodist Church daycare. I had battled depression my whole life but this time was the worst. I couldn't make sense of my feelings. I had this anger that wouldn't let up. I wanted to kill people. That became my mantra. I want to kill you. Suicide was never far from my mind either. I was staying busy now just to keep from acting on that thought. I hated everyone except my children. Matt, Ashley, Andy and my little chihuahua, Abbie, had my entire heart. The rest of the world could collapse for all I cared. I had to watch over these last three children I was blessed with even if they were grown. I had so much guilt bearing down on me for slaughtering my other children. I had to make up for that.

Ashley and Mickey had gotten into a fight one night over her not having a job as well. She was still in high school and we didn't have an extra car but once Mickey started fussing about a subject he didn't let up. He was drinking more and he was unbearable when he got ticked off. He loved to talk and he always had to have the last word when he had some alcohol in him. Ashley finally had enough and told him to F off. She called my oldest daughter to come and get her and she left that night. She was going to move back in with James. Things were never the same between me and Mickey after that. My guts were churning and having one of my children leave made it worse.

My past weighed heavily on my mind. I couldn't sleep at night because of the onslaught of memories. Mickey's drinking was getting worse. He would start at 10 in the morning and wouldn't stop until he passed out. The sweet man I knew had turned into an alcoholic. An addict like every other man that I crossed paths with. I remembered a time when all I heard were the kindest words from him. Now all he did was gripe and groan and tell me what a mistake he made by marrying me. He never missed a chance to shove my face into the mud verbally. Once again I was backed into a corner and I had no more options.

Larry died on October 12, 2010. His parents had died within months of each other and Larry followed soon after. He died in that house that he ran like a prison all alone. His oldest son, Todd, had found him 2 weeks after his death and got in touch to let the rest of us know. The way he died says a lot about the kind of man he was. He was determined to destroy lives and push people away. He could have sought help but he chose to keep the cycle of abuse going. For years I wondered how I would feel when I got the news. I always assumed Larry would outlive me. Usually the meaner you are then the longer you live but I was still standing after the hell Larry had put me and my kids through. Larry left everyone out of the will except for the kids from his first marriage. I contested the will. They were his kids and deserved something for the nothing that he gave them when he was alive. Larry's daughter wouldn't budge and I had a lien put on the house. The houses that Larry and his parents had so much pride in have been collapsing since. The grass has grown up so high you can't even see either of them.

The windows have been broken out by teenagers or homeless people. The walls all have holes in them. It's amazing that either of them is still standing. Those houses have been full of bad memories and destruction and pain for so long. Now they're only monuments to rot. I know I shouldn't say it but the world is a tiny bit better with those Finneys in the ground.

Ashley thrived moving back home. She got a job at a local restaurant and James bought her a little yellow Volkswagen beetle. James reveled in giving her more than I could and putting me down. He told her what an awful mother I was. He told her I was a slut and he loved to call me trailer trash whenever the opportunity presented itself. He left his house and everything else he owned to Ashley in his will. He gave Hope $100 because she had his last name when she was born but he made no provisions for Matt or Andy because they stood by me. I decided that I was going to leave Mickey. I didn't know where I was going to go but I couldn't take being berated by him anymore. I was so rattled from being hollered at by him that I thought I was going to have a nervous breakdown. I was on my way home from work one evening when I stopped by the library. There was a local magazine called Journey that had Christian themes. I took it home with me and after supper I was looking through it and came across an article that said, "Do you need healing from an abortion?" A light came on for me. I didn't know anyone would talk about this subject, let alone print a story in a magazine. There was a number to call but when I picked up the phone I put it back down again. I couldn't go through with actually reaching out for help. After a few more sleepless nights, I called. I was nervous and shaking but the woman on the other end was very kind. She told me when the next meeting was and I made plans to attend.

The meeting took place at the woman I talked to on the phone's apartment in Montgomery. There were 6 of us there and we all introduced ourselves and talked about our abortions. I was the only one that had multiple abortions. The counselor, Sherry, pulled me aside and told me she wanted to start seeing me one on one. For the next 9 weeks I started attending her classes. I was given a workbook to study in and a Bible. I hadn't opened a Bible in years. The work took time, effort and commitment. It drained the life out of me and there were times when I saw how this could possibly help me but I had to finish this. I couldn't go on like I was. I went once a week after work to meet with Sherry. I couldn't sit still talking with her. I moved around the room anxiously and I would physically groan. I learned that this was my way of keeping my feelings repressed. I had buried these thoughts so deep in my heart and now I had to dig them up again.

The tasks in the workbook were a struggle uphill. I didn't want to look back at what I had done all of those years ago. My mind would go blank. I would close the book and then start a fight with my husband just to distract me. Through the homework I discovered post-abortion syndrome. The symptoms may not appear until years later, making it difficult to diagnose. Some of the symptoms include: outbursts of anger, difficulty maintaining relationships, anxiety attacks, aggression, suicidal thoughts and sexual promiscuity. They all fit me like a glove. There were times when I would go see Sherry and we couldn't even have a session because I was so emotional. I was rumbling inside. I was a volcano ready to erupt at any moment. I continued with the work and would get so disgusted with myself that I would throw it across the room and swear that I wouldn't go back. Mickey didn't understand any of this. He told me that if he had known I aborted my children then he wouldn't have married me in the first place. He was drinking like it was the end of the world everyday now. I couldn't look at him anymore. The only love I felt was for my children and my precious chihuahua Abbie. I built a wall between me and everyone else. I was running on bitterness and hate. There wasn't room for God in my heart, not while the devil took up residence inside of me.

Driving home was an ordeal for me. If another driver did the tiniest thing I would fly off the handle. I wanted to run them down and make them pay. I was drowning in a sea of rage and I couldn't find the shore if I wanted to. Every week, when I was supposed to have a session with Sherry, you could count on me self-sabotaging. There was always a fight with my husband, a problem at work or I wasn't feeling well. There were so many times I showed up at Sherry's with my car packed with my belongings. We spent the time of our sessions talking about my marriage instead of getting to the underlying issues. Sherry would talk me down and then I would be stable enough to drive home. I continued with the work, slowly but surely, and I was starting to see the light.

One day I called Sherry and I asked her to pray for me. I was understanding the Bible more and more and the work we were doing was finally making sense. In the middle of her prayer I could feel bile creeping up my throat. Strong and wretched and I couldn't keep it down. I started throwing up this green sludge. I don't know how else to describe the vomit. I couldn't believe this had come from inside of me. I told Sherry what happened and she said it was demonic. I had been in the devil's grip for so long and he didn't want to let me go. I didn't let this deter me. The more work I did, the more clarity I got. I could understand all of those years of anger, bitterness and hatred. I had been like Rachel in Jeremiah 31:15. I had been in mourning and great weeping for my children and refusing to be comforted.

During the class Sherry gave me a piece of paper and told me to write down all of the name of the men I had sex with. She told me this would be a private matter between me and God. When I was done , she said a prayer breaking the connection I had to them. We went onto the balcony and burned the paper in a metal bucket. While the paper was turning to ashes she told me to ask God to reveal what my children were. I spent a lot of time praying for the answer and then it came to me suddenly and felt like knowledge that had been carved right into my heart. I had two boys and two girls. We gave them birth certificates and had a memorial for them. I named them Sarah, David, Aaron and Mary. A name gives life and restores dignity and it brings order out of chaos. John 10:3 says that. He calls His own sheep by name and leads them out. A day will come when I meet these babies and explain what happened and why. I'm no longer afraid of that day. I will hold them in my arms and love them completely and I will be loved in return.

Once I finished with the classes I was a changed woman. I knew Jesus and I wanted to live for him. I wanted to help other women that might've been in the same position as me. I started speaking at local churches and sending my testimony to Christian magazines, radio and TV stations. I was fortunate enough to be published in a few of them and I started appearing on some radio shows. I was also a guest on a television show just outside of Atlanta. All of those years ago I went there to abort my son but now I was here sharing God's grace. During the filming one of the crew members actually started crying. She was the camera woman who had an abortion when she was younger but told no one. The night I was on the show was too much for her. She had to walk off because she was so upset. As soon as the show was over the producer who invited me on the show asked if I would speak with her. She was in the lobby and she was inconsolable. I told her the rest of my story and then I told her to take it Jesus. He was the only one that could take her pain away and give her forgiveness. She hugged me and told me she was going to do exactly that. I felt so lucky to be able to do this for others. To help them see what had taken me so long to see. I knew this was what I wanted to do. I wanted to help others feel God's love. The shackles of the past were gone but it wouldn't be long before turmoil found its way back into my life.

Mickey had been bitter about me speaking at churches and getting involved with pro-life. He complained about being home alone all the time but whenever I was home all he wanted to do was get drunk and fuss. Mickey had a friend named Herbie that moved in next door and I knew he was going to be trouble. He was an ex-trucker and an awful person through and through. He was the black sheep of his family. His father owned a landscaping business and a lot of land around Wetumpka. He even donated several acres to the city. Herbie and his father didn't get along so he was left to his own devices out here in the woods. He was a short, overweight man with white hair and a matching goatee. His voice was all nasal. It came solely out of his nose and every word was rushed. He sounded like a drunk auctioneer. My husband started spending all of his time with this man. Mickey said they were friends from way back but he had never talked about Herbie before and Mickey talked about everyone. I had a terrible feeling about this man right away.

He started lying to me about where he was in the evenings. I had to find out from my other neighbors that he would go to Herbie's from 4:30 to 6:30 because he knew I would be at work and wouldn't know. Young girls came in and out of Herbie's house all the time and he would provide them with drugs in exchange for sex. I didn't want Mickey around that, like any other wife, but Mickey would holler and fuss and tell me that I wasn't his momma and that he could see his friend whenever he wanted. This man was driving an even bigger wedge between me and my husband and I didn't stand a chance, apparently. There was a time when Mickey stayed up at Herbie's past midnight and when he came home he was out of his mind. He was shaking and told me that his truck was possessed. I knew Herbie had given him something so I waited until he eventually went to sleep and I took his cell phone and called Herbie to say thank you for giving drugs to my husband. Mickey's weight practically fell off of him. He wasn't sleeping, he had no appetite and he would sweat profusely. I waited until he went to bed another night and that's when I snuck into his truck and found a pipe and a baggie full of what looked like tiny pieces of broken glass. I didn't know what it was. I had to go on the internet and search and eventually found out that it was crystal meth, the most addictive of all drugs.

He spent even more of his time at Herbie's and before long he was using drugs again. He had a history of drug use many years ago but I thought he had put all of that behind him. He started using marijuana when he was a teenager well into his 30s but he stopped when he had a heart attack. He was a full blown alcoholic but I knew how to deal with that behavior. I couldn't believe it when I found out.

Mickey would work from 6 to 4 as a mechanic at a gravel pit. When he got off he would stop at Herbie's and, after hours of drinks up there, he would come home and do yard work. He would rake leaves until 1 in the morning. Somehow he could never get tired. He couldn't sit still even if he wanted. I found out quickly that meth addicts make great landscapers. The yard would be spotless and Mickey would still find a reason to be out there. This went on for months before he started cutting the grass at night using a flashlight. The only time he ever seemed to rest was when he was doing meth in his truck. I confronted him constantly about his drug use but he would deny my accusations. He said I was crazy and then went back to what he was doing. Those were the only times that we would talk. He started taking over an hour getting high in the morning before work. He couldn't even make it to his truck before he had to get in and fire up again. I couldn't imagine how much he was doing all day when he was at work. His drinking didn't let up either. He had a cooler full of beer that he kept with him in his truck and he couldn't even wait until he got home to start cracking them open. On his way home he would polish off a 6 pack. He didn't have any feelings anymore. All he cared about was getting high, staying high and hanging out with Herbie.

The first time I actually caught Mickey doing drugs was when he was in Herbie's backyard. My son, Andy, was home and told me that Mickey had been up at Herbie's since he got off work. Herbie wasn't home but Mickey was still there sitting in his truck. I had just got off work myself. I don't know how he didn't see me drive past him. I cut across the prison field so I wouldn't be seen. I snuck up on Mickey and as soon he realized I was there he panicked. He threw whatever he had in his hands underneath the seat. I asked him what he was doing and he said nothing. I told him that I knew he was doing drugs and he didn't say a word. I told him that he wasn't fooling anybody. Mickey kept insisting that I was crazy but that word didn't affect me like it used to. He had been calling me that for so long it had lost its sting. I told him that I was going to turn Herbie in and Mickey said that I would be messing up a lot of lives if I did that. I told him that I didn't give a damn. Herbie had messed ours up from top to bottom and he laughed the entire time he was doing it. I couldn't have sympathy for this man or anyone associated with him. This wasn't the first time we'd had this argument and it wasn't the last time he would show his devotion to Herbie but when I was walking away I knocked over all of Herbie's patio furniture. It made me feel a little bit better.

    The dirt road turned into a war zone after that. Herbie would push my buttons and I would lash out and all of our neighbors got to hear us airing our dirty laundry while we fought on the front porch. Herbie was always crossing the line, testing his boundaries and he knew what he was doing the whole time. I had told Mickey that he and Herbie could do whatever they wanted when I wasn't home. Mickey let me know he wasn't going to give this man up for anything but I didn't want to see the two of them together when I was around. The sight of Herbie turned my stomach but the man didn't know when to stop. He started coming down whenever he pleased. He knew when I got home from work and could've got away from the trailer before I got there but it was like he timed it out to make sure that I knew he was here. His faded out Mustang would creep down our driveway and him and Mickey would go drink and blare rock music while they sat in lawn chairs in our storage house. I went to tell Mickey that supper was ready and Herbie was sitting there with his chest puffed up and grinning from ear to ear. I told Herbie that he needed to get out of here but he said he wasn't going anywhere and then he called me the B word. I couldn't believe the gall of this man. He acted like he was untouchable. I thought this would've been enough to actually make Mickey mad. I couldn't imagine another man being able to hear someone else call their wife that and not do something but Mickey lowered his head. He didn't say a word. Mickey never liked confrontation unless he was fighting with me but he was the biggest coward when it came to Herbie. I knew right then that was the moment I no longer had my husband. I left the storage house with a fury that would drive me completely. I knew I had to take this man down somehow.

Herbie had another trailer tucked deep in the wood behind his house that he rented out. A man named Darren was living in it and he was the one who was cooking meth. He had been arrested in another county and somehow made his way here and now he was the one making most of the meth in Elmore county, it seems. I couldn't go to the gas station in our town without seeing people that were as hooked as my husband. At night there was a carousel of cars coming through. They'd drive down to the hill behind Herbie's house and exit through the gate on the other side. It reminded me of lines at McDonald's. All you could see were headlights and all you would hear would be bass music loud enough to rattle the windows. Every Thursday, when my husband got paid, he was making the trek down the hill to load up. Weight was falling off of him. He started to look like an AIDS patient. He looked like a shrunken head attached to a stick figure. He had to buy his clothes in the kids section because that was all that would fit him. I would brush against him in bed at night and start crying because the way he felt reminded me of my sister before she died.

I called the cops to come patrol our road all the time. More and more cars were coming and going at all hours of the night. A party was happening 24/7 at Herbie's. Mickey stayed glued to the kitchen window, peeking through the blinds and wishing so badly that he could be there. When he was finally liquored up enough to go to bed, I would call the cops and turn out all the lights at our house and watch Herbie and his gang panic. I would go out on the porch and when the cops went to turn around, I would stand at the edge of the road and flag them down. I told them all about what went on at my neighbors house and they said they knew. They said it was clear as day what was going on but they needed a reason to stop the cars that were leaving so suddenly. I would have to be patient but it was worth it to watch

Herbie squirm. He turned the music off and cut off all the lights at his house and stopped the traffic from coming in and out. I could count on him talking to my husband and I would get chewed out for going against my husband's friend but I loved raining on their parade. I knew Herbie wouldn't control my life forever.

It was raining hard on my way home. I could barely see the road with the way it was pouring. I reached the dirt road and the mud was especially nasty. The red clay mush stuck to everything. I had to wash my car daily just driving normal down the road because the dust was so thick out here. I kept my speed safe and slow because I didn't want to have to get out in the storm and hose the mud off but then I saw headlights approaching fast in my rear view mirror. I knew it was Herbie's car and he was almost ramming into the back of me. He was in a hurry to get home but I was in the way. He decided to pull around me and cut me off but when he did he came within inches of taking the front off of my car and sending me into a ditch. He raced to his trailer and I followed after him and that's when I saw my husband's truck parked in front. My husband was in Herbie's living room with some 20-something year old girl. They were sitting close on the couch and she was one of Herbie's girls, that's for sure. Scrawny and barely dressed and her eyes made her look like she was a million miles away even when she was right in front of you. Mickey came out like nothing had happened. I went to tell Mickey about what happened on the road but Herbie got to him first. Herbie told Mickey that I was trying to run him off the road and Herbie's word was good as gold. I didn't stand a chance in this fight. Mickey had thrown me to the wolves for his drug dealer. I added this night to the list of things I couldn't bring myself to forgive him for.

The financial hole that Mickey had been digging with his drug use had almost swallowed him completely. He was having to take more meth because his tolerance had built up and his paycheck wasn't covering what he needed to get by. He had to start charging more on his cards. He would go to Lowe's and buy something frivolous so he could get a couple hundred dollars in cashback. When he hit his limit there then he would go over to Wal-Mart and do the same thing. He mostly bought Herbie groceries but a lot of the time he was buying tons of meat for the two of them and whatever girls Herbie had over to feast on over the weekend. He was doing this 3 or 4 times a week. He left one of his Wal-Mart bills on the table and I took a look at it and the balance was in the thousands. All the money we had was literally going up in smoke. Our pantry and refrigerator were empty. Food didn't matter to Mickey. He lived off of meth and alcohol and when he did feel like eating it was only pizza rolls. He would finish working in the yard at 1 in the morning and then he would come in and make a giant plate of pizza rolls only to fall asleep with them in his lap. I would wake up in the morning and they would be scattered all over the floor. Mickey kept our expenses down to the bare minimum. We didn't have air conditioning or heat. We had an ancient window unit for the summer but Mickey hardly let me run it no matter how sweltering it was. In the winter, we only had portable heaters but he would fuss so much about the power bill that I didn't want to use it. A kerosene heater had to get us through. It could be 20 degrees outside and Mickey would insist that it wasn't cold. He was sweating so much from all of the drugs that the weather didn't phase him. Aside from buying Herbie groceries, Mickey started paying the bills for this man. The light bill or his speeding tickets and whatever else this man needed. He had to make sure that he had food and electricity because if he didn't have those then the girls wouldn't stick around. They were only around for the good times but the second they couldn't eat or have a place to charge up their phones then they were hitting the road. Herbie couldn't stand being alone and there wasn't anything that my husband wouldn't do for this man. When Mickey was tapped out on cashbacks and his paycheck, he started taking out loans. He got them to pay off his Wal-Mart and Lowe's bills and to help finish off what was left on my car payment. He paid off half of each but none of it went towards my car. Instead he spent it all on drugs. An entire $20,000 loan was gone in a few weeks and he was left with an $800 a month payment for it. He went right back to running up his cards. The debt just kept building and building. He would blow up when the bills came but when the anger burned off he would run back and borrow more money. The amount of meth that he was doing at this point was staggering. We were in the dead of winter and he stayed out most of the night burning pine straw and lighting up his pipe. He would come in stinking of smoke and hop right in the bed. He stopped showering and taking care of himself. I kept waiting for the night that he wouldn't come in at all and I'd find him dead in the dirt. I kept waiting for the hammer to fall and for our lives to come apart completely.

An old friend of Herbie's and Mickey's just happened to live down the street from Ashley. Her name was Jeannie and she was with the same party crowd as Mickey when he was in high school. She ran with his circle and becoming a mother and grandmother hadn't helped her grow up much. She was a meth addict and before long she was up at Herbie's every night. The two of them were in some kind of meth wonderland up there. They were playing house and doing drugs and Herbie was so happy to learn tha Jeannie lived so close to my daughter's house. He was going to use her to finish tearing me and my husband apart. Ashley had developed Rheumatoid arthritis and made it difficult for her to get around. My sons and I helped out with whatever she needed and that meant most weekends were spent over there. Before long Jeannie was driving past the house in her jacked up SUV and seeing what all we were doing there. She drove so slowly she might as well have parked out there and took notes. She would see me taking the garbage out and stare like she'd never seen another person do this before. She started regularly patrolling the block and I had no idea what she was doing until I went home and Mickey was accusing me of seeing another man. I told him where I was and he was more than welcome to drive over and see for himself but he believed whatever Jeannie had told Herbie. She started taking pictures of my car and then leaving no-so-subtle hints that she was around. One time I found an empty bottle of Mickey's Full Malt liquor tossed in Ashley's yard because she knew I would find it. Jeannie's harassment got to the point where I had to finally threaten to get a restraining order against her. I didn't even know this woman and I had to go to such lengths to get rid of her. The fights at home were getting worse. Somehow all of this was still my fault. Mickey just couldn't see why I had such a problem with his friends. He said we should all learn to get along and have a good time together. Mickey's whole mission in life was to have a good time. He wanted a woman that was like the ones that Herbie had going in and out like a revolving door. He wanted a woman to smoke and drink with. He didn't want a woman who cared about family and the church. Every good memory that he had involved him either drunk as a skunk or so high he might never come down again. He was a hard worker and could've had more than a collapsing trailer off a dirt road but his bad habits were dug in so deep. He wanted his life to be a never-ending party and now he had nothing to show for it.

After a while Mickey started using marijuana again. His dealer from way back lived down the road from us and Mickey started going to him to load up. His name was Shaw and he was the long haired, long bearded hippie type. He didn't have a license and couldn't drive so he sold weed out of his mother's old house. Mickey would do favors or run errands for Shaw if he didn't have enough that particular week. Usually it was taking him to buy groceries but if the local fair was in town then Mickey had to take him so he could stock up on carnival food. Shaw would buy a whole freezer full and wrap them up and save them. He would live off of conecuh hotdogs and funnel cakes for weeks. One time on my way home I saw Mickey on top of Shaw's roof putting up Christmas lights. I guess even people who sold drugs liked to get into the Christmas spirit. Mickey would come home and the entire trailer would reek of weed. Mickey would be in the bathroom sitting on the toilet hunched over like a gargoyle. His drug bag, which used to be a shaving kit, was on the floor filled with a mix of what he got from Shaw and Herbie. The stench and the smoke from the marijuana was so dense it was like walking through a sauna. I asked Mickey, "How much is enough? How high do you have to be?" He couldn't answer me and when he did answer me all he would do is just deny it. He didn't smell anything and his friends weren't drug dealers and he wasn't doing anything wrong. He would tell me that he got up and went to work and he paid the bills. That was all that mattered. I didn't understand why he had to live in a haze of drugs. All I heard from the time we met was how he came from this wonderful family and how he was so lucky to have grown up the way he did. He was over at his mother's house doing chores his brothers and sisters didn't want to do, working like a dog for them, and I didn't understand how they couldn't see that something was wrong. The fact that he looked like a skeleton should've tipped them off. Everyone commented on his weight and asked him if he was sick but he would shrug it off and say that he was taking diet pills. I reached out to Mickey's sister to have her help me get him into rehab but she didn't believe me. She said she needed proof so that's what I gave her. I sent her pictures of Mickey's stash and a video that Andy had taken of Mickey smoking meth right in our driveway. She said she was horrified but she couldn't help me. She loved her brother but couldn't confront him with this. I didn't understand it. If you loved someone then why would you let them continue on like this? He wasn't going to listen to me but I thought if he had help from his mother or his brothers and sisters then he would have a chance. I ran into a dead-end again.

When Mickey didn't have enough meth or weed he got violent. He would shove me into the wall or against the window in the kitchen. There were so many times I thought he was going to hit me. He would call me the B word and tell me that I ruined him. He told me to get out. He told me that was what Herbie wanted too. He would get high the next day and forget that he even said these things. When he was coming down he turned into a demon. I cried. I prayed Mickey would get caught. I knew that was the only way Mickey would stop. This went on for 3 years and my blood boiled the entire time. I could've killed Herbie myself. This one man had caused all of this hell and destruction. I finally went to see a lawyer about a divorce. I couldn't cope with it anymore. I prayed to God for direction.

On November 9th, I woke up like any other morning. I got up at the same time as Mickey and helped get him out the door. Before the drugs, I used to make him breakfast and we would watch the news together until he had to leave and then I would go back to bed. These days I mostly just got up out of habit and Mickey spent most of the morning locked up in the bathroom using. That morning was different though. There was no garbage pickup where we lived so Mickey would take it with him and put it in the dumpster at the gravel pit. I was getting the garbage ready to be taken off. I was tying the garbage bag up when Mickey finally came into the living room. I asked if he was taking the garbage off and he said no. He had put this off for a couple days and I asked why. Mickey told me that he wasn't going to work. I pressed him and he told me that he had been fired 2 weeks ago and he had been arrested. My stomach felt like a cold river was running through it. Rough, unforgiving water was sloshing in my guts. I dropped what I was doing and asked Mickey to repeat what he said and when he did it didn't make any more sense than the first time he told me. He relayed the story slowly to me. His job was located on prison land and when he got to the entryway two cop cars were parked and they had a drug dog with them. The cops didn't stop any of the other workers except Mickey. They made him turn off his truck and asked him if he had any drugs on him. He told them that he only had marijuana on him but the drug dog sniffed out the meth and the pipes that he had hidden in the cab. They arrested him and took him to jail that morning.

Mickey's sister bailed him out and he had been hiding all of this from me. He had been getting up every morning and leaving and going and sitting at his older brother's house until he knew I was gone so he could come back home. His addiction had taken what little we had and now we had nothing at all. I was beyond livid. I was the one on the warpath now. I marched to the front door and went out onto the porch and Mickey bolted after me. I kept asking him how could he do this to us? I had been asking it when each piece of the life we had was taken away but now we hit bottom. I repeated the question but he wouldn't answer. He could hardly look at me. I stomped off the porch and started towards Herbie's house. I told Mickey I was going to kill this man. I didn't know how I would do it but this anger, this hatred was an inferno inside of me. Herbie had slowly but surely wrecked my entire life. Pulling a whole world apart was a punchline for him and at that moment I couldn't abide him living. Him drawing another breath seemed like the most offensive thing that I could think of. I didn't make it off of the porch before Mickey was grabbing me, holding me still, fighting not to let me go. He knew I meant what I said but I don't know if he was holding me back because he didn't want me to deliver on my promise or because the thought of harm coming to Herbie was too awful of a thought. Mickey had to get me in a bear hug to keep me from getting loose. I wriggled like an eel, dying for a moment to get away. Mickey told me to calm down, he said it was going to be okay but I couldn't see how. He didn't have a job, he probably couldn't find another one and he was facing jail. I fought against the clenching arms of Mickey when all of a sudden Herbie's car came rolling slowly right in front of our house. Mickey signaled for him to leave but Herbie parked right next to Mickey's truck and got out. He seemed to want a front row seat to the fight we were having before the sun was even up. I'm not proud of the words I used but I couldn't help myself.

The anger was immense. I had been holding it back for so long and the dam was broken now. Mickey had to become a human wall in between us. I lunged and swung, I was clawing at the air trying to get to Herbie. I'm sure I looked feral but I wanted nothing more than to harm this man, if you could even call him a man. Herbie got the message quickly and stepped back and went to his car. Mickey pushed me back as far as he could and he told me to stop. He looked me in the eyes and told me that it would all be okay. He stood there and I knew he didn't believe a word he was saying. His eyes gave him away. There was desperation radiating off of him. He wanted nothing more than to get off of this porch and go get high somewhere else. It killed me watching him walk away so easily from this. The way he put drugs first even when he had just hit rock bottom. He went to his truck and fired it up and peeled out angrily. He kicked up dust in the frigid winter air. He followed Herbie's car down the road and all I saw were taillights. I don't know where they were going but I stood out there for the longest time looking at the road. I didn't feel cold, I didn't feel anything. I'd been brought so low by Mickey over the past 2 years that I seemed incapable of crumbling. I knew that he would have to get help now and actually face his demons but I knew he'd go fighting tooth and nail to hang onto his habits. At leastI knew his family couldn't turn a blind eye anymore. They would have to see the wreck of a person that I had been dealing with on my own. I went back into the house and I dried my eyes. I steadied myself and then headed towards the bedroom to get ready for work.

The weeks after Mickey's arrest were especially awful. Without the drugs to keep him in a zombie state, he lashed out at me more than ever. We couldn't speak to each other without him accusing me of being the one that had turned him in. Mickey's older brother knew Mickey's boss at the gravel pit and the two of them talked after his arrest. He asked why Mickey was fired and his boss said that all of the workers were complaining about the stench of marijuana and how long it took him to finish one job. He noticed how much weight he lost and how Mickey would be fixated on one task and get nothing else done for the day. His boss had enough of it and didn't have much choice. Mickey didn't want to hear that though. He was convinced that I was in good with the police and I was conspiring with them to bring him down. He went on and on about how I wanted so badly to bring down Herbie but I got him instead. The fact that he still had the nerve to mention the name of the man who put us in the situation surprised me but I wasn't sure why. Mickey getting arrested didn't seem to damage their bond whatsoever. You would think they had saved each other's lives at some point with how close they were. He wore blinders with Herbie, he couldn't find fault with this man if he wanted to, and the finger was pointing back at me. Nothing had changed.

Mickey was out of work for 3 months. He was half-heartedly looking for work. His brother knew a man that owned several local gas stations and was trying to get Mickey on with him. The man hired several addicts in the past and gave them a chance to turn their lives around. Mickey was going to go around to other stations in the area and fix broken pumps and repair signs. He would start immediately if they needed help but he had to be ready. He got up in the morning and went over to his brother's house and waited until around noon and then he came home and drank himself to sleep. His sister had to give him a loan to pay our bills and buy groceries for all of the time he was out of work. Mickey didn't seem like he was particularly interested in getting another job. Without the meth making him think he was Superman, he started to ache all over again. He wasn't up until 3 or 4 in the morning doing yardwork. His appetite came back and the weight that practically fell off of his bones was sticking to him now. He was starting to become the man that I fell in love with. He finally found a job at the gravel pit that he worked at when we first got married. Our lives were slowly becoming normal again but Mickey's sentencing loomed over us.

The cost of Mickey's bail, the lawyer, those months he was out of a job, plus all of the money he owed to Wal-Mart and those loans he took out when he was high, meant that he would never be able to retire. He didn't know whether he was going to jail or not but he knew that he'd work until he died to try and undo mistakes of his addiction. We kept waiting for Mickey's day in court but it never seemed to arrive. Months went by before he even got summoned to court and even then he didn't get sentenced. The lawyers still had to be paid and Mickey's family was hounding him, especially his sister, to stay on the straight and narrow. Mickey didn't know that I had reached out to his sister and tried to get him some help and she hadn't told him either. I resented her and his entire family for not stepping up when Mickey needed them the most and helping him before he threw his life away. He didn't understand why I wasn't more grateful to Jane for helping us get by all of those months he was out of a job but he didn't know his sister the way I did. She thought she could buy her way out but you can't absolve yourself of addiction. She would have to look in her brothers eyes forever and know deep down she could've done more.

When Mickey had his day in court he was sentenced to 9 months of community service, AA meetings and he had to attend weekly counseling sessions. A much lighter sentence than we were initially thinking since the law in Alabama was being harsh on narcotics related charges. It felt like we could finally take a breath. We knew it'd be a lot to work through but at least prison wasn't hanging over our heads anymore.

God's Grace Alone

Herbie came out of all of this unscathed. Girls came and went and the meth dealing never halted for a second until Herbie's father died. He left Herbie out of the will but left behind homes scattered all over the county for his other children to divide for sale or to keep. Herbie's older brother let him stay in a house that was located in one of the more run down neighborhoods. He packed up and left Darren to keep the drugs running. Darren stuck around until his girlfriend Lisa overdosed and that's when he decided to call it quits. Herbie quickly moved another couple in and then another couple once they didn't work out either. Business seemed to be taking a bad turn for the man who thought he was untouchable for the longest time. Without Mickey, his best customer, around to cater to his every need, the tie that kept them bound to each other was coming undone. I hoped every bridge between the two of them would be burned and I'd never have to hear or see this man again for the rest of my life.

Not long after Herbie left, my dog, Abbie, started getting sick. She had always been a chunky little thing. She might've been a chihuahua but she had quite the appetite and I always did spoil her. I got her from the wife of James' brother and this tiny dog had a terrible life before she ended up at my door. She had been passed around from family member to family member, had been hit, never really shown any love, and when she was a puppy someone sat on her leg and they never bothered getting it fixed. She walked around on her 3 legs with her injured one drawn up. She was a skinny, nervous dog when I found her and didn't seem to like much of anyone but she took to me immediately. I fell for her just as quickly. She became my shadow and my fiercest protector. She loved my kids but everyone else needed to earn her trust when it came to me. When Mickey was in the heaviest parts of his drug addiction he couldn't even come near me without her barking or growling at him. She sensed his demons and didn't want him any closer. She was a chihuahua who thought she was a German shepherd when it came to watching over her momma. When I was working she couldn't stand being away from me. She would settle down and nap all day, conserving her energy until I walked through the door and then she was all over me. Circling my feet with her little tail wagging and begging for me to pick her up and love on her. A lot of people say their animals are like their children but Abbie always seemed more like a person than a dog. She had so much personality behind those dark bulging eyes of hers. I adored her and wanted to make her the happiest dog in the world. Things were normal until she started throwing up. I didn't think much of it at first because I figured she'd just eaten something that didn't sit right on her stomach but then it started happening after every meal. Money was still tight and I couldn't afford to take her to the vet so I had to borrow money from my kids to have the doctors look at her. They looked into her diet and wanted me to stop giving her junk food and she also had a stomach infection. She was put on pills and they hoped it would clear up but her age was also a factor. Abbie was 16 years old and getting to the age where she couldn't fight this off. My heart crumbled. She was losing weight quickly and the pills didn't seem to be helping. She all but stopped eating and the energy just drained out of her. It got the point where she couldn't even stand up to go to the bathroom. We had to kneel down and hold her sides because her bony legs couldn't support her anymore. She slept and shivered all the time. I kept an eye on her stomach rising and falling to see if she was still alive. I knew she was miserable and I did everything in my power to make sure she was happy and comfortable and tried to cherish the time we had left because I knew she wasn't long for this world.

On Easter of 2019 Abbie died. We were in bed together and she was sleeping right next to me under the covers. I had gotten up early and I was just looking at this little dog that had brought so much light to my life and she was looking right back at me. She reached out and put her paw on my thigh and then she drew her last breath. I was in absolute agony. I've had other dogs in my life and I loved them but none were like Abbie. I had to get my sons to take her body away. I couldn't bear to see her like that and I couldn't bring myself to touch her. We buried her in the backyard at Ashley's house in the corner where she loved to sniff and mark her territory. We built a cross for her and put a statue of a chihuahua with angel wings on her grave. Each day without her has been a struggle. I don't know what to do without my shadow and her nails clicking on the floor behind me but I know I'll see her again. She'll be there on the other side waiting for me with her tail wagging a hundred miles an hour. I can't wait to pick her up and hold her again.

I had lost one angel but another was on the way. Ashley had gotten pregnant and I was overcome with joy. She had so many health problems that I thought that wasn't in the cards for her but then we were all preparing for the arrival of this beautiful baby boy.

On November 19th, 2019 Avery Micah was born. The labor was tough on Ashley but so worth it to see her hold this sweet child in her arms. She took to motherhood instantly and I couldn't be more proud. I broke down the instant he looked at me. The sight of this big eyed boy with chubby cheeks that would put a squirrel storing food for the winter to shame became my new happiness. He felt like the prize waiting at the end after all of the years of struggle. I thank God for every moment that I get to have with him.

My life has been slowly piecing itself back together after being fractured for so long. Mickey and I are still working on our marriage. He still drinks but hopefully through counseling he can find out exactly why he has these compulsions. Herbie is probably off causing destruction somewhere but I know he'll have a lot to answer for when his time comes. My kids and my grandchild are happy and healthy and I have no one to thank but God himself for that. My journey has had countless stumbles and I'm not proud to say that I've had doubt in my heart but He has never once faltered. I've been torn open and I've howled like an animal at the moon with my voice shot through

God's Grace Alone

with pain but He took his hand and used it to guide me in from the wilderness. I'm not the little girl left to die under the house all of those years ago. He took this broken thing and used her as a vessel, as a witness, and I want to be a shining example of His love. I know now that because of Him I'm not alone. I know now that I never was. He has always been beside me.

www.ingramcontent.com/pod-product-compliance
Lightning Source LLC
Chambersburg PA
CBHW071759040426
42446CB00012B/2631